Arab Friends, Neighbors, and Guests

A Study Guide for Christians

Katy Abdallah

Augsburg Fortress
Minneapolis

Contents

Arab Friends, Neighbors, and Guests
A Study Guide for Christians

Writer: Katy Abdallah
Contributors: Dora Johnson, Janet M. Corpus
Editors: Laurie J. Hanson, Jill Carroll Lafferty, Andrea Lee Schieber, Julie Lindesmith
Designer: Alan Furst
Cover Designer: David Meyer

Developed in cooperation with the Division for Congregational Ministries of the Evangelical Lutheran Church in America (ELCA), David Poling-Goldenne, project manager.

The script on the cover and at the top of each page can be translated as "Welcome."

Manufactured in U.S.A.

ISBN 0-8066-4447-8

05 04 03 02 01 1 2 3 4 5 6 7 8 9 10

Our Arab Friends: An Introduction

This resource is intended to provide a thumbnail introduction to Arab peoples, cultures, and religions so that you and your study group can begin or strengthen the process of welcoming in your congregation and understand what individuals of Arab heritage bring when they enter your community or congregation. Another purpose of this resource is to encourage people who are of Arab heritage to share their faith stories. The specific goals of this resource are:

- to outline a biblical and cultural basis for hospitality to your Arab neighbors.
- to learn about the diversity of Arab cultures, peoples, and religions in the Arab world and in the United States.
- to gain a sense of the commonalties between Arab American and dominant U.S. culture and of the contrasts that can enrich us all.

Who?

Though the group using this resource may vary in size from perhaps 6 to 12 people, it's important to include a wide variety of people

and to include some congregational leaders such as a pastor and outreach ministry leaders—those involved in worship, evangelism, social ministry, and community activities. After these sessions have ended, find ways to share the knowledge and experience acquired in this study with more people in your congregation.

Arrange for each group member to have a copy of this book. A layperson or pastor can lead the sessions, and leadership need not be limited to one person.

Your group will be immeasurably enriched by the participation of at least one Arab American participant. If it is possible, invite one or two Arab Americans to one or more sessions. If it is not possible to have Arab Americans participate in these sessions, invite one or more Arab Americans to join you in conversations or to make a specific presentation at a later date.

Where?

The environment of your sessions can help teach the hospitality this study hopes to convey. Be sure the space is set up ahead of time with adequate lighting and ventilation. Have the seating arranged in a circle or around a table, with the flexibility to allow for the smaller group conversations that are part of the sessions.

When?

This book contains ample material for four to eight sessions, each one to two hours in length. A meeting time other than Sunday morning might be best. Near the end of this introduction, you'll find suggestions for alternative ways of structuring your use of this resource.

Only the facilitator has regular session preparation that must be done. Group members are asked to journal daily throughout the series, and this journaling will provide the basis for some of the discussions.

Session 3 includes recipes for preparing a meal that your group can enjoy together during the last session.

What?

Each session includes the following components:

- Overview—gives a summary of the session and its goals.
- Materials—lists what you will need for the sessions.
- Preparation for facilitator—identifies tasks that must be done prior to meeting.
- Opening—gathers participants in devotions.
- Community building—engages participants with one another.
- Bible study—lays a biblical basis for the session's topics.
- Exploration—invites participants to explore attitudes and experiences.
- Cultural close-up—provides information (and, in some cases, exercises) to deepen knowledge and understanding of Arab Americans.
- On hospitality—provides discussion questions or exercises for reflecting on hospitality practices.
- What's next—gives an assignment that prepares you for the next session or the next steps for your congregation to become more welcoming to Arab Americans.
- Closing prayer—prepares the group to go out.
- Going further—lists additional resources.

How?

Read through the sessions to begin thinking about the best format to use for your setting. This study is prepared for a series of at least four two-hour sessions. This will be time well spent in learning about the heritage of your Arab friends, neighbors, and guests. Below are some alternative ways to use the material in a more time-restricted format. In general, you can gain time by asking some or all of the group members to read the "Cultural Close-Up" sections ahead of time. Also, in cases where both small group and plenary discussion is recommended, you may choose to do one or the other.

For a series of four one-hour sessions

In addition to overall preparation, the facilitator will read and prepare the material presented in "Cultural Close-Up." An alternative to this is to have group members take turns sharing this responsibility. Another option is to ask everyone to read the "Cultural Close-Up" ahead of time, with different members of the group responsible for presenting the information each session. During the course of a session, this information can be presented at a specific time or shared throughout the session as appropriate and necessary. For each session, you will need to focus on either the "Bible Study" or "Exploration" portion.

For a series of eight one-hour sessions

In this time frame, it will be possible to focus on both the "Bible Study" and "Exploration" components.

For an unrestricted number of sessions

Your group may choose simply to work through the material page by page for as many sessions as this takes.

For a retreat or weekend intensive study

Use each session in its entirety for a day's segment. For example, you may have four sessions: Friday evening, Saturday morning, Saturday afternoon, and Sunday afternoon.

Common ground

Learning about a different culture is bridging a divide that demands listening and sharing skills. You may want to discuss the following at the beginning of the series or review it at the opening of each session. If possible, use these statements to make a poster that will hang prominently in your meeting space.

- We are all God's children.
- We will show hospitality and welcome one another just as Jesus Christ has welcomed us.
- We will listen to one another.
- We will respect one another's questions.

The facilitator can read over this list and then ask, "Can we all agree that this is our common ground for today's conversation?" Have the group discuss any questions or comments that arise. This common ground will help you look at habits, language, and cultural orientation of people from another culture.

1

Hospitality

Overview

Hospitality—welcoming the stranger—is at the core of the study and work to which this book invites you. Take an honest look at the ways you open yourself to people you may not know or understand. In the process, you will grow in understanding how to extend hospitality to others whose habits, language, and culture are not your own.

In this session, you will:

- learn about the biblical virtue of hospitality.
- grow in empathy toward those who are strangers to you.

Preparation for facilitator

Read the entire session ahead of time and gather the materials. Read the overall introduction to this series. If you will not have enough time to use all the materials presented in this session, the introduction makes suggestions about how to decide what portions to use.

Materials

For this session, each member of the group will need a copy of this study, a Bible, a pen or pencil, and a blank name tag. The facilitator will also need chart paper or a board and markers.

Opening

The facilitator will guide the group through the following meditation: Sit comfortably with your eyes shut. Remember an occasion when you met a stranger. This person may have been someone to whom you were introduced or someone you saw across a room or walking down the street, someone you liked or someone you feared. Take a few moments to focus on the person. Get as clear an image as you can.

Hold this person in your imagination as you listen to some Bible passages. *(Read Romans 15:7 and Hebrews 13:1-2 aloud slowly, pausing between them.)* Now imagine that person as a messenger from God. *(Pause for a few moments.)* What does this messenger from God have to say to you? *(Pause again.)* Let us pray. Loving Creator of us all, guide us as we learn to welcome your children who may be new and even strange to us. Hold us together in your love. Amen

Community building

Make sure everyone has a blank name tag and a pen or pencil. Choose someone you don't know well to be your partner for this activity. Take two minutes to introduce yourselves and make name tags for one another. Then return to the group and introduce your partner to the rest of the group.

When introductions are complete, name the categories of information you gave in making introductions. List these on chart paper.

Bible study

In the Bible, hospitality is an active virtue. Read Genesis 18:1-16. Read verses 1-8 and 16 again. Note the ways in which Abraham and Sarah show hospitality:

- Upon seeing the strangers, Abraham does not wait but goes out to meet them.
- Abraham greets them respectfully with a bow.
- Abraham invites them to have a drink, wash their feet, and rest from their journey.
- Abraham and Sarah offer them bread for refreshment.
- Abraham refers to himself as their servant.
- Abraham engages the servant in showing hospitality.
- Abraham and Sarah provide not only water and bread but also meat. Indeed, they provide the best—"choice" flour, "a calf, tender and good," curds, and milk.
- When the strangers leave, Abraham goes out with them "to set them on their way."

1. Based on the example of Abraham and Sarah, name some of the dimensions of hospitality.

2. Share ways in which you show hospitality. What are the similarities and differences in how you show hospitality, compared to Abraham and Sarah and among members of the group? Which differences are more personal, and which are more cultural?

3. Abraham and Sarah showed hospitality to complete strangers. To whom do you show hospitality? Share any experiences when you have shown hospitality to strangers.

4. Hospitality is based not only in the stranger's need but in our own, not only in the stranger's experience but in our history. Again and again the Hebrew scriptures called upon ancient Israel to remember who they had been—and call upon us to remember who we have been. Read Leviticus 19:33-34. Try rephrasing these verses to apply to you and your community's history. Who in the group—or whose forebears—were newcomers to the community and had the experience of being the stranger? Name ways that those experiences are related to welcoming strangers today.

5. Showing hospitality to others is showing hospitality to Jesus. Read Matthew 25:31-46. Jesus mentions strangers together with those who are hungry, thirsty, naked, sick, and imprisoned. Count off by fives to assign each person to one of the categories on this list.

a. Put yourself in the position of a stranger. Take a few moments to meditate on what you would experience as a stranger who is hungry, thirsty, naked, sick, or imprisoned. How do you feel? How do others respond to you?

b. How did you become a stranger who is hungry, thirsty, and so forth? What are your needs? What are your gifts?

c. How do we usually treat strangers? Is there anything we should do differently?

d. What is Jesus' relationship to those who are hungry, thirsty, naked, sick, imprisoned, or strangers?

e. Now share your thoughts about this with the group. Make a list of responses on the chart paper or writing board.

f. Next to the first list, make another list of ways to welcome strangers.

In *New Testament Hospitality: Partnership with Strangers as Promise and Mission* (Fortress, 1985), Bible scholar John Koenig notes the importance of strangers who we meet for the first time in

the three biggest Christian festivals: at Christmas, the child; at Easter, the traveler whom the disciples meet on the road to Emmaus; and at Pentecost, the Holy Spirit. Koenig points out that in the Bible, Jesus is often in need of hospitality. For example, Jesus has nowhere to lay his head (Luke 9:58). Then, in situations where he is the guest, the tables are turned and he becomes the host.

6. Divide the following Bible passages among members of the group: Luke 5:29-39, 7:36-50, 10:38-42, 11:27-28, 14:1-24, 19:1-27, and 24:13-35. Reflect on these questions as you read your passage. Then share responses in the large group.

a. What kind of hospitality does Jesus seek in this story?
b. How does his host respond?
c. How does Jesus become the host?

Exploration

Have two volunteers read the following dialogue between Amal, an Arab woman, and Emily, a Euro-American woman, meeting each other for the first time.

Amal: How do you do? My name is Amal. I am from Jordan, but we are really Palestinians.
Emily: Hello! I am Emily.
Amal: Are you from here?
Emily: Yes.
Amal: Are you married?
Emily: No.
Amal: Do you have brothers and sisters?
Emily: Yes, a brother and a sister.
Amal: I have 10 brothers and sisters.
Emily: That's nice.
Amal: What does your father do?

Emily: My father was a butcher.
Amal: Oh, what does he do now?
Emily: He died three years ago.
Amal: Oh, I'm so sorry. May God rest his soul. (She lays her hand on Emily's arm.)

After hearing the dialogue, discuss the following questions.

1. Which questions seem familiar and normal to you? Which strike you as unusual?

2. What would be your first reaction to these questions from a person you have just met?

3. How would you be likely to respond?

Context is an important part of getting to know someone. In dominant U.S. culture, first meetings commonly elicit questions such as, "What do you do?" and "Where are you from?" People from Arab cultures are likely to ask questions that help them understand their relationship to a person they have just met. Other questions Arabs might ask when they first meet a person are about one's religion, status in the community, extended family, and marital status. Many people in the United States aren't accustomed to hearing these kinds of questions from someone they've just met. Arabs also will not necessarily shy away from religion, politics, and money—issues that many people in the United States treat almost as taboo. We can view such differences as barriers or we can view them as gifts.

4. For further exploration, form small groups of three to four people to discuss the following questions.

a. Describe an encounter you had with someone from a cultural background different from your own. What were the differences? What images did that encounter produce for you?
b. In what ways does your congregation show hospitality to visitors? In what ways does your congregation show hospitality to

residents of the surrounding community? Would your congregation be welcoming to someone of Arab background? Why or why not? (You may not feel you know enough to answer. Take some guesses. Over the coming weeks, you will gain more insight.) Record your responses and guesses.

Cultural close-up

Reflecting on hospitality

Parker Palmer, who writes and teaches about community, points to the stranger as spiritual guide. In Genesis 18, you read the story of God's messengers who come as strangers to Abraham and Sarah. Not only may God's messengers be strangers—the stranger may indeed be God!

After Jesus' crucifixion, two grieving disciples traveled on the road from the capital city Jerusalem, where Jesus had been tried and executed, toward the village of Emmaus. They had lost not only their friend but also their hope in God's promise of liberation. On the road, they met a stranger who revived their hope. That stranger was the risen Jesus. Experiencing God's power of life over death, the disciples returned to Jerusalem, their hope restored (Luke 24:13-35).

In both the story of Abraham and Sarah and the story of the disciples on the road to Emmaus, hospitality opened the door to the knowledge of God's presence, promise, and power. In *The Company of Strangers* (Crossroad, 1985), Palmer writes that this role of "the stranger in our lives is grounded in a simple fact: truth is a very large matter, and requires various angles of vision to be seen in the round. It is not that our view is always wrong and the stranger's

always right, but simply that the stranger's view is different, giving us an opportunity to look anew upon familiar things" (pages 58-59). In fact, Palmer argues, God is such a stranger "who continually speaks truth afresh, who continually makes all things new. God persistently challenges conventional truth and regularly upsets the world's ways of looking at things. It is no accident that this God is so often represented by the stranger, for the truth that God speaks in our lives is very strange indeed. . . . God uses the stranger to shake us from our conventional points of view, to remove the scales of worldly assumptions from our eyes" (page 59). Yet, as the late pastoral theologian Henri Nouwen wrote, our feelings toward the stranger are very ambivalent.

1. Think of a time when you encountered a stranger whose way of doing things or seeing things was different from your own. Name words that describe how you felt.

2. Think of a time when you resisted a stranger because the person's views or ways of doing things were different from your own. What was it that put you off? List words that describe how you felt.

3. Now list how you wish you had felt. How might you have responded differently?

4. Think of a time when you were a stranger to others. How did you feel in that experience? How were you treated?

5. Think of a time when you welcomed a stranger and were enriched by the experience. Try to name how you felt. What in particular was a gift to you in that experience?

In *Reaching Out: The Three Movements of the Spiritual Life* (Image Books, 1966), Nouwen writes that welcoming the stranger involves creating a free and friendly space in ourselves. Creating this space, says Nouwen, is not easy. It requires commitment, focus, and work.

We need to free ourselves from deeply ingrained habits of response—and non-response—in our encounters with strangers.

Palmer adds that the stranger is also important because faith is a journey. Faith takes us to new places where we are ourselves strangers. Palmer writes that all of us who yearn for God's promises fulfilled, God's "kingdom come on earth as it is in heaven," are journeying strangers in this time and place where we wait and watch.

Our mobile society also makes strangers of us. The ancient Hebrew people were nomads but they traveled as a community. We move individual by individual and household by household, alone. And if we don't move, our neighbors do. As neighborhoods change around us, we may become strangers in places we have known well and called home for much of our lives.

Globalization, immigration, and new technologies mean massive ongoing change for us and for our neighborhoods.

6. How are globalization, immigration, and new technologies affecting your community—your congregation, the neighborhood of your congregation, and the neighborhood in which you live?

7. What effects do these changes have on how familiar you are with those you meet at work, at school, shopping, or on the street?

8. How do you feel about these changes?

God called the ancient Hebrew people to wander toward promises and new life, says Palmer. "Could we not see our own situation in this same light? Is it not possible that the social upheavals of our day—our own sense of being exiles on earth—are God's way of calling us into a new future, away from the divisions of the past toward a holy city? . . . What a curious inversion—taking feelings of estrangement which we normally try to get rid of and calling them positive signs of vocation instead" (pages 62-63).

9. Recall, if you can, a time when a stranger brought a message important to you or the situation you were in.

Arab hospitality

Hospitality is a prime virtue among Arab peoples. It's not surprising that Arab cultures hold this value in common with ancient Bible stories. Some Arab cultures, and the Arabic language itself, developed in the same geographic region where the Bible stories were told and written down.

Arab peoples are well known for their generosity to guests. Hospitality is important to one's reputation and standing and is shown not only in homes but also in shops and offices. Like Abraham and Sarah's welcome to their visitors, Arabs welcome guests expected or unexpected, convenient or not. Welcoming guests, offering seats, and offering something to drink are key components of Arab hospitality. A host will often offer the best seat to a guest. Meals are prime opportunities to show hospitality and generosity.

The guests' reciprocal and hospitable response is to receive these offers of welcome. For example, guests always accept the offer of refreshment even if they take only a sip of what is offered.

1. How are these traditions of hospitality similar to or different from what you're used to as a host and as a guest?

2. Name one- or two-word phrases describing your congregation's hospitality.

3. How are these Arab traditions of hospitality similar to or different from the ways your congregation shows hospitality to visitors? Consider specific situations such as worship, Sunday school, and coffee or fellowship time. How are people greeted upon their arrival at your site on Sunday morning or at other times?

4. Name the specific ways in which God is the host of Holy Communion in your congregation. Think about this in concrete terms, for example, who invites you to the meal? Where is it? Who

sets the menu? Who prepares the meal? How is it served? What are the roles of the servants and of the guests?

5. How does thinking about congregational visitors as guests affect your ideas about appropriate welcome and hospitality?

On hospitality

The Arab expression *inshallah* has many and varied uses. Here are some to illustrate its meaning. In each case, what's most important is that *inshallah* defers to or prays for God's will.

A pregnant woman is wished an easy birth: *Inshallah* you deliver safely.

To the couple after their wedding: *Inshallah* we come on happy occasions.

On a new year: *Inshallah* you live for more good new years.

Congratulations on moving to a new house: May God make it blessed, *inshallah* you see God's goodness in it.

Wishing a person who has worn or bought new clothes or footwear: Congratulations *inshallah* you wear it on good occasions; *Inshallah* you buy one hundred dresses; *Inshallah* you wear it in good health; *Inshallah* you wear out its threads and may you enjoy it.

Referring to someone seriously ill: *Inshallah kher,* I hope it will end well.

What's next

Keep a journal during this study. You may choose to write extensively or to write just enough to help you remember your thoughts. Here are some suggestions:

1. Jot down Bible stories about hospitality. How does each story relate to being hospitable today?

2. If you are not of Arab descent, write about any personal encounters you have with Arab persons. What do you learn in these encounters? If you are of Arab descent, write about encounters in which you become aware that you are Arab. What do you learn in these encounters?

3. Note stories you hear about Arabs or the Arab world, including newspaper or television stories. (You may want to cut out newspaper articles.) What images do these stories evoke?

4. Make a note when a friend, relative, colleague, or other acquaintance mentions anything regarding Arabs or the Arab world. What images do these comments evoke?

Closing prayer

Welcoming, embracing God, teach us to welcome the stranger as you have welcomed us. Give us insight, honest conversation, and open minds as we focus on our Arab neighbors. Teach us to listen and speak in ways that reflect your love revealed in Jesus Christ. Amen

Going further

Film

View the movies *Babette's Feast* (G, 1987) or *Soul Food* (R, 1997). How does hospitality at a meal draw people together? What are the implications for hospitality in your community?

Books

Keifert, Patrick R. *Welcoming the Stranger: A Public Theology of Worship and Evangelism.* Minneapolis: Fortress Press, 1992.

Nouwen, Henri J. M. *Reaching Out: The Three Movements of the Spiritual Life.* New York: Image Books, 1975. See especially the second section "Reaching Out to Our Fellow Human Beings—The Second Movement: From Hostility to Hospitality."

Palmer, Parker. *The Company of Strangers: Christians and the Renewal of America's Public Life.* New York: Crossroad, 1985. See especially chapters 1 and 3, "Life Among Strangers—An Introduction" and "A Spirituality of Public Life: The Stranger as Spiritual Guide."

2

The Arab World and Arab Peoples

Overview

The Arab world encompasses a vast geographic expanse and diverse peoples and cultures. Learning about that diversity is not only part of breaking down stereotypes, it is also part of learning the richness of our global and local neighbors' heritage.

In this session, you will:

- learn about the diversity of the Arab world.
- reflect on prejudices about Arab people.
- learn to address stereotypes.

Preparation for facilitator

Read the entire session ahead of time and gather the materials. If you will not have enough time to use all the materials presented in this session, see the introduction for suggestions about how to decide what portions to use.

Materials

For this session, each member of the group will need a copy of this study, a Bible, and a pen or pencil. The facilitator will also need chart paper or a board and markers.

Opening

Since the first session, you have kept journals related to hospitality and to experiences with Arab persons and the Arab world. Take a few moments to recall your journaling over the past week. Then, if you wish, offer one-sentence prayers related to your journaling. Pause between prayers and be sure to allow time for anyone who wishes to pray. When all prayers have been offered, pray the following prayer together aloud:

Gracious and loving God, be with us today as we learn about our brothers and sisters. Open our hearts and minds to you and to one another. Help us to let go of stereotypes and to see all people—especially now Arab people—as your beloved children. Amen

Community building

In the last session, you introduced yourself to someone you didn't know well. Today, pair with another person you don't know very well. Get acquainted with each other by sharing responses to the following questions.

1. Where were your ancestors from? If they were not native to North America, when and under what circumstances did they come here? If they were native, what was their experience of being in this country?

2. What do you know about your ancestors' origins? What else would you like to know about your ancestors?

Bible study

The Arab world is home to Muslims, Jews, and Christians who share a common heritage, as well as other smaller groups. Two lineages from Abraham—one with Egyptian Hagar and one with Hebrew Sarah—were the forebears of the Arab and Jewish peoples. Jesus' followers made up a sect that split from Judaism in the first century of the Common Era. Islam began in the sixth century.

Read Genesis 16:1-16 and 17:1-8, 15-22.

1. What is the relationship between Sarah and Hagar at the opening of the story? How does that relationship change?

2. Compare the promises that the Lord made to Hagar (16:10-12) and to Abraham concerning Sarah's offspring (17:15-16).

3. What is the relationship between Hagar and Sarah's offspring in the promises the Lord makes to Abraham (17:1-8)? Consider this question both from the Lord's point of view and from Abraham's point of view. (At this point in the story Abraham does not expect offspring with Sarah.)

4. How do the following promises to Abraham affect the relationship between Hagar and Sarah's offspring? The Lord said, "I will establish my covenant with him [Sarah's offspring, Isaac] as an everlasting covenant for his offspring after him. As for Ishmael [Hagar's offspring], I have heard you; I will bless him and make him fruitful and exceedingly numerous; he shall be the father of twelve princes and I will make him a great nation. But my covenant I will establish with Isaac, whom Sarah shall bear to you at this season next year" (17:19b-21).

The Qur'an teaches that Isaac's line developed the faith of Israel and that of Christianity while Ishmael's line developed Islam. The faith of the elder son Ishmael is seen as the true faith of Abraham and more universal.

5. Compare what you have read and discussed so far in this session to the following passage from the Qur'an. How is this similar to what you have been reading? How is it different? What does it say about the relationships among Islam, Judaism, and Christianity? What does it say about the relationships among the people it names?

> "Say, 'We believe in Allah, and in what has been revealed to us and what was revealed to Abraham, Ismail; Isaac, Jacob, and the Tribes, and in (the Books) given to Moses, Jesus, and the Prophets, from their Lord: We make no distinction between one and another among them, and to Allah do we bow our will (in Islam).'"
>
> —Sūrah 3:84

6. Now read Genesis 21:8-21. What do you imagine was the relationship between Ishmael and Isaac? How did the relationships among Abraham, Sarah, and Hagar affect the children's relationship? If you were one of these parents, how would you explain to the children why they were separated? What insight, if any, does your response provide into how we deal with the separations between Muslims, Jews, and Christians?

Exploration

Brainstorming gets varied responses on the table to help our thinking. The facilitator asks group members to respond to a question, a word, or an idea. Group members respond quickly, saying whatever

comes to their minds. The facilitator records responses. No one comments. There are no right or wrong answers in a brainstorming session.

1. Brainstorm responses to the following: What stereotypes do people around the world have of people in the United States? Record responses on the chart paper or board.

2. When you are done, read the list. Mark each stereotype positive (+) or negative (-). Go through the list again, marking each item true (T) or false (F).

3. Next, write down on the chart paper or board all the nationalities you can think of that speak Spanish.

Important cultural differences distinguish the nationalities that speak Spanish. The same is true of Arabic. The Arab world includes parts of North Africa, touches Asia Minor in the north, and spreads to the African Sahara desert in the south. Arabic is the official language in 21 countries.

4. For each item on the following list, note the first word that comes to mind. Be honest—the very first word. You won't be sharing these words with others.

- Arabs
- Arab men
- Muslims
- Good Arab
- Arab women

Turn to page 35 at the end of this session and compare your responses with the results of a survey conducted by the Arab American Anti-Discrimination Committee.

5. Now as a group, list positive stereotypes about Arabs or Arab culture on the chart paper or board.

It is very possible that you are able to list fewer positive stereotypes than negative. We live in an environment where many powerful negative stereotypes of Arab people blind us to the reality of who Arab people really are. Some of the positive stereotypes used to describe Arab people are: hospitable, generous almost to a fault, industrious, good humored, scrupulously honest, politically oriented, friendly, patriotic, family oriented, religious, helpful, loyal, community minded, and endowed with a zeal to make the world around them a better one without letting go of the past.

Cultural close-up

The word *Arab* refers to the variety of peoples who share language and, to a lesser extent, history and culture. *Arab* does not refer to a racial or national group. With its location on two continents and along a coastline with access to vital waterways, the Arab world sits on one of the most strategic regions on earth.

This region has fertile agricultural lands and beautiful mountain ranges, such as the Atlas range in northwest Africa and the Lebanon range in southwest Asia. While some areas enjoy considerable amounts of rainfall, humidity, and occasional snowfall, dry climates are more prevalent. Water resources are crucial. Most settlement is in high densities along the coastline and rivers, for example, along the Nile in Egypt and the Tigris and Euphrates in Iraq.

It was here that human beings first established a settled form of society, cultivating grain and raising livestock, establishing cities, and developing diverse skills and occupations. Ancient Egypt, Sumer, Assyria, Babylonia, and Phoenicia are among the rich and complex cultures that flourished. Archaeologists are uncovering more and more traces of these ancient civilizations throughout the region.

Diversity characterizes the Arab world, a rich composite of many influences. Diverse ethnic, linguistic, and religious groups inhabit the region. The region's geography includes urban centers, as well as isolated rural areas.

The following is a very brief glimpse of the diversity among Arab nations and their peoples. Margaret K. (Omar) Nydell's book, *Understanding Arabs: A Guide for Westerners* (Intercultural Press, 1996), provides a fuller picture not only of topics touched on here, but also of other aspects of the Arab world and its peoples.

Government

From the late 13th until the early 20th century, members of the House of Osman, the Ottomans, ruled the vast Ottoman Empire centered in what is now Turkey. At its height in the mid-1500s, the empire extended from the Balkan Peninsula to the Middle East and North Africa. After a slow decline, by the 20th century the Ottoman Empire was much smaller and weaker, beset by internal and external conflicts. World War I marked the end of the Ottoman Empire. In fact, some Arab groups aligned with Europeans against the Ottomans in the hope of overthrowing their rule. Rather than achieving independence, however, in 1918 much of the dismembered empire was divided into colonies or territories of France, Britain, Italy, and Spain. So began Arab struggles for national independence, which various states achieved, primarily in the 1950s and 1960s.

The governments of Arab nations are varied. There are monarchies, for example, in Morocco, Jordan, Kuwait, and Qatar. Algeria, Libya, Egypt, Syria, and Yemen have socialist governments. These governments can be described in various ways, such as authoritarian, elite, benevolent, liberal, or democratic. In some nations, Islamic fundamentalist movements are gaining political as well as social influence.

Language

While Arabic, which originated in the Arabian peninsula, is the primary language of 21 nations, many people in these countries are multilingual. In Morocco, Algeria, and Tunisia, the schools teach both Arabic and French. In northern Morocco, Spanish is also common. In Lebanon, people with more education speak French, English, or both, along with Arabic. English is the most common second language in Egypt, Iraq, Jordan, Bahrain, Qatar, and the rest of the Arabian gulf.

In addition to Arabic and European languages, many people in the Arab world also speak local languages. In Algeria, where Arabic is the native language of only about 80 percent of the population, many speak native Berber or both Berber and Arabic. Armenians in Lebanon speak Armenian in addition to whatever other languages—Arabic, French, or English—they may use. Syrian minorities speak Kurdish, Turkish, Armenian, Syriac, and Aramaic. Kurdish is also spoken in Iraq. In Sudan, Arabic is spoken by only about 40 percent of the population, while more than 100 native languages are spoken.

Ethnicity

Ethnic diversity characterizes the Arab world. A significant portion of Algeria's population is descended from native Berbers. This is true in Morocco, too, where there are also many people of sub-Saharan African descent. The populations of Tunisia and Libya are of mixed Berber and Arab background. Iraq's population is about 71 percent Arab and 18 percent Kurdish. The remaining 11 percent includes Turks, Assyrians, Armenians, and some people of Iranian origins, as well as other ethnic minorities. In Jordan, about five percent of the population is Bedouin (native tribal nomads) and there is a significant Palestinian population, mostly refugees from Israel/Palestine. In

Sudan, people in the north are primarily Arab while the south is primarily African. There, as elsewhere in the Arab world, ethnic differences have sometimes meant civil strife.

Population

Egypt has the largest population of any Arab nation, with approximately 65 million people in 1995. It also has one of the highest population densities in the world. By contrast, Sudan, which has the largest land area of the Arab nations, has a population of about 29 million and a relatively low population density. Morocco has about 29 million people and one of the highest population growth rates in the world. The smallest populations are in Qatar and Bahrain. About half of Bahrain's 500,000 people live in the capital city. Qatar's population of about 400,000 is double what it was in 1949 when oil was discovered.

Economy

Oil comes to mind when we talk about the economies of the Arab world—and for good reason. The Arabian Gulf area has the largest oil and natural gas reserves in the world. Iraq, Kuwait, Saudi Arabia, Bahrain, Qatar, and the United Arab Emirates are oil rich. Kuwait's oil wealth gives it a per capita income among the highest in the world. Within 15 years of the beginning of oil production in 1946, poverty was virtually eradicated in Kuwait.

Formerly a nation of farmers and semi-nomads, Libya saw its revenues multiplied 20 times over by 1969, eight years after oil was discovered. Oil income has meant a rising standard of living for all economic classes, along with improvements in nutrition, health care,

education, transportation, and communications. Today the economy is almost entirely dependent on oil.

In the case of Iraq, U.S. and United Nations embargoes have turned oil wealth into hardship. The sale of oil had accounted for 95 percent of foreign exchange earnings. The international embargo reduced that figure to less than 10 percent, which has affected education, health care, nutrition, and virtually every aspect of life.

Algeria is the world's largest producer of liquefied natural gas, and other income is derived from oil, mining, and agriculture. Algeria imports most of its food, though it was once agriculturally self-sufficient.

Some of the Arab states continue to maintain agricultural economies. Two-thirds of Algeria is part of the Saharan desert, but there is excellent agricultural land in the northern coastal region. Algeria is the world's largest exporter of phosphates. About half of Morocco's population is engaged in traditional farming. Agriculture, tourism, and phosphate mining are the economy's base. Tunisia, too, has good agricultural land in the north. About a third of the population is engaged in agriculture. Tunisia's economy depends on agriculture along with tourism and some oil and natural gas production. In Oman, more than half of the population works in agriculture. Farmers make up about a third of Syria's population. Oil, phosphates, and textiles are also important to the economy. Intensive agriculture in Yemen makes coffee and cotton big revenue sources.

Bahrain's economy is diverse, including dry dock services, aluminum production, light engineering, banking, and tourism. Egypt's economy is based in oil, cotton, other agricultural products, and tourism, and depends heavily on U.S. aid. Jordan's diverse economy includes tourism, mining, industry, trade, and agriculture.

The status of women

Although stereotypes about the status of women in the Arab world abound, in this area as well as virtually all others, diversity is characteristic. Tunisia leads the Arab nations in liberalizing traditional social values. Most women wear Western clothing and many are well educated. They are more and more active in the labor force, for example, in education, social services, health care, and office administration. In Egypt, women have participated throughout the workforce for many years. Many Egyptian women have stopped wearing the *hijab* or headscarf. Women in Lebanon participate in professions, commerce, and social organizations, though traditional values are more restrictive in rural areas.

For at least a generation, women in Syria and Iraq have been well educated and participate in the labor force as teachers, social workers, and health care workers. Public education for all children since the 1960s means the participation of women in the labor force is on the rise. Jordanian women, who are also becoming better educated, make up a significant percentage of the labor force. Most are teachers, clerical workers, or health care providers. At the same time, education does not guarantee employment or an active life outside the home. In Sudan, most women are now being educated, but few work outside the home, even in urban areas.

In some Arab nations, women are severely restricted. In Saudi Arabia, women are fully covered in public. They cannot travel alone, which means they cannot drive cars. Those few who work outside the home must be in all-female environments. Kuwait is much like Saudi Arabia in these respects, though women and men may work together. In Algeria, where family and social traditions are very conservative, women are not as active in the labor force and more wear the *hijab* than in any other North African country.

Yemeni women were in 1993 the first women in the Arabian Peninsula to vote in a national election. Still, the status of women in Yemen varies widely. In the north they are veiled in public, have little education, and rarely work outside the home. In the south, women have equal status under the law and work in varied fields, including accounting, mechanics, and factories.

Where women are less educated and less active in the workforce, marriage is an important factor. For example, in Qatar more than 80 percent of women marry between 15 and 20 years of age; in Oman, women usually marry by age 18.

Religion

The next session deals with Arab religions more fully. Here is just a glimpse of the diversity of religions in the Arab world.

Although the majority of Arabs who have immigrated to the United States are Christian, Islam is the dominant religion in the Arab world. Morocco, Algeria, Tunisia, Libya, Egypt, Iraq, Saudi Arabia, Yemen, Kuwait, Bahrain, and the United Arab Emirates are 95 to virtually 100 percent Muslim. Saudi Arabia is where Islam was born, and Iraq is home to important sacred sites.

Yet, there is religious diversity both among different religious groups and among sects within Islam. Among Muslims the major sects are *Sunni* and *Shiite.* Most are Sunni, and there are large Shiite populations in Lebanon, Iraq, and the Gulf states. Other Muslim groups include Alawites (an eighth of the population of Syria) and Wahhabi. The Druze religion, derived from Islam, is present in Lebanon, Syria, and Palestine.

In both Morocco and Tunisia, amid populations that are 98 to 99 percent Muslim, there are Christians of European background as well as Jews. In Egypt, where Islam is the official religion, about 94 per-

cent of the population is Muslim. The remaining population is made up of native Christians, mostly Copts. The largest Christian populations are in Lebanon (30 percent) and Syria (10 percent). Most Lebanese Christians belong to the Maronite rite, a native Lebanese denomination. Indian Hindus have lived in Oman for centuries.

Local religions are also important, for example, in Sudan about one-quarter of the population adheres to indigenous religions (about 70 percent are Muslim; five percent, Christian).

On hospitality

1. If you are hosting a new immigrant unfamiliar with your culture, would it be better for you to:

a. find out about the person's culture and try to be hospitable in ways that the person is used to?
b. be hospitable in your own familiar ways?

2. Explain your choices. What are the benefits and risks to each approach?

What's next

Use your awareness of stereotypes about Arabs to promote greater understanding in your congregation and community. Make a commitment to do one of the following this week:

1. I will tell a friend or coworker about this session's conversation about stereotypes.

2. When I hear someone talking about Arab people in stereotypes, I will address the stereotype with that person.

3. I will teach a child something I learned in this session about the diversity of the Arab world.

4. Learning to address stereotypes in ourselves and in others is a process. In preparation for acting on your commitment, imagine what it will be like. What might you say? What are your hopes and fears? How will you respond to the other person's response? Expect that in fulfilling this commitment, you will learn more. You may be surprised at what you learn from the other person.

Closing prayer

Gracious God, your creation speaks of your majesty and might. Help us to see all people as your children. Keep us from judging others. Lead us to welcome strangers and to learn from them new ways to give you honor and glory. We pray in the precious name of Jesus. Amen

Going further

Books

Fernea, Elizabeth Warnock and Robert A. Fernea. *The Arab World: Personal Encounters.* Garden City, N.Y.: Anchor Press/Doubleday, 1985.

Hourani, Albert. *A History of the Arab Peoples.* Belknap Press of Harvard University, 1991.

Itzkowitz, Norman. *Ottoman Empire and Islamic Tradition.* Chicago: University of Chicago, 1972.

Nydell, Margaret K. (Omar). *Understanding Arabs: A Guide for Westerners.* Revised edition. Yarmouth, Maine: Intercultural Press, 1996.

Puthiyottil, Cherian. *Our Neighbors: An Introduction to Cultural Diversity and World Religions.* Minneapolis: Augsburg Fortress, 2001.

Raheb, Mitri. *I Am a Palestinian Christian.* Minneapolis: Fortress Press, 1995.

Said, Edward. *Orientalism.* New York: Vintage Books, 1979.

Compare your responses

The Arab American Anti-Discrimination Committee conducted a survey of print media, television, and movies. Compare your responses to the "Exploration" on page 25 with the following stereotypes found in the survey.

Arabs: "Ay-rabs," camel jockeys, towel heads, sand niggers, Muslims, Arabian nights, Sheik, harem, desert, camels, Bedouins.

Arab men: oil sheiks, fabulously wealthy, lavish and wasteful, buying up America, greasy merchants, swarthy, dirty, greedy, unshaven, uneducated, dishonest, manipulative, incompetent.

Muslims: fundamentalists, extremists, militants, fanatics, terrorists, cut off hands, oppress women, *jihad* as "Holy War."

Good Arabs: minor character, passive, culturally Western, dramatically insignificant, subordinate to Western heroes, never the main character or action hero.

Arab women: oppressed by Arab men or by Islamic beliefs, confined to home, veils, head coverings, long robes, passive, uneducated, voiceless, faceless, characterless.

3

Arab Culture and Religions

Overview

Amid diverse ethnic groups, Arabic as a common language has created many aspects of common culture.

In this session, you will:

- learn about Arab culture and religions.
- experience points of connection between U.S. and Arab cultures and between Christianity and Islam.
- plan to prepare and share a meal of Arab cuisine.

Preparation for facilitator

Read the entire session ahead of time and gather the materials. If you will not have enough time to use all the materials presented in this session, see the introduction for suggestions about how to decide what portions to use.

Materials

For this session, each member of the group will need a copy of this study, a Bible, and a pen or pencil. The facilitator will also need chart paper or a board and markers. Though not necessary for the session, it would be helpful to have a copy of the Qur'an available.

Opening

Pray the following prayer aloud as a group.

In the name of the Father, Son, and Holy Spirit,
Praise be to God
The Nurturer and Sustainer of the World;
Most Gracious, Most Merciful;
Lord of the Day of Judgment.
Thee do we worship,
And Thine aid we seek.
Show us the straight way,
The way of those on whom
Thou hast bestowed Thy Grace,
Those whose portion
Is not wrath,
and who go not astray.
Amen

Then look on page 38 at the prayer from the Qur'an:

Al Fātihah (The Opening)

In the name of Allah, Most Gracious, Most Merciful.
Praise be to Allah
The Cherisher and Sustainer of the Worlds;
Most Gracious, Most Merciful;
Master of the Day of Judgment.
Thee do we worship,
And Thine aid we seek.
Show us the straight way,
The way of those on whom
Thou hast bestowed Thy Grace,
Those whose (portion)
Is not wrath,
And who go not astray.

—Sūrah 1.1-7

1. How is this prayer from the Qur'an similar to or different from prayers used in your congregation?

Pray together: Gracious and loving God, it is your will to hold all creation together in your love. Help us to see what we humans have in common and how we differ, and to celebrate both to your glory. Amen

Community building

Form groups of three or four people each to review "What's Next" from the last session. What did you notice in stories and comments about Arab people or nations? What commitment did you make to promote greater understanding in your congregation or community? What did you do? Describe the experience.

Bible study

Abraham's encounter with the Lord gives some insight into an aspect of Middle Eastern culture and relationships: diplomacy and negotiation. Read Genesis 18:17-33.

1. How many times does Abraham appeal to the Lord?

2. How would you characterize each of the following aspects of the negotiation?

a. Abraham says, "Will you indeed sweep away the righteous with the wicked? Suppose there are fifty righteous within the city; will you then sweep away the place and not forgive it for the fifty righteous who are in it?" (vv. 23-24).

b. Abraham says, "Far be it from you to do such a thing, to slay the righteous with the wicked, so that the righteous fare as the wicked! Far be that from you! Shall not the Judge of all the earth do what is just?" (v. 25).

c. The Lord responds, "If I find at Sodom fifty righteous in the city, I will forgive the whole place for their sake" (v. 26).

d. Abraham says, "Let me take it upon myself to speak to the Lord, I who am but dust and ashes" (v. 27).

e. Abraham says, "Oh do not let the Lord be angry if I speak . . . Let me take it upon myself to speak to the Lord . . . Oh do not let the Lord be angry if I speak just once more" (vv. 30-32).

f. Abraham says, "Suppose five of the fifty righteous are lacking? . . . Suppose forty are found . . . thirty . . . twenty . . . ten" (vv. 28-32). (Why do you think Abraham didn't go any further?)

g. The Lord responds, "I will not destroy it if I find forty-five there . . . For the sake of forty . . . I will not do it, if I find thirty there . . . For the sake of twenty . . . For the sake of ten" (vv. 28-32).

3. How would you describe the relationship between Abraham and the Lord?

Share how situations of negotiation and diplomacy in our lives are similar to and different from that between Abraham and the Lord.

Read Genesis 23:1-20.

4. What is the object of negotiation in this story?

5. What is the dimension of hospitality in this encounter?

6. How does Abraham's grief figure in this story?

7. How do the parties show one another respect? How do they communicate their desires and intentions?

8. What do you think? Should Abraham have accepted the Hittites' offer of the land as a gift?

9. How is the diplomacy in this story similar to or different from your own experience?

Exploration

Exercise 1

Many English words have their origins from Arabic. Here is a list of Arabic words. Sound them out as best you can. Try to figure out what the English cognates are. Some of the meanings are included as hints. Answers can be found on page 48.

1. Al-Kahf (cave)
2. Al-Jabr
3. Ardi Shokeh (ground plant with thorns)
4. Barriah (wilderness)
5. Kahwa
6. Koton
7. Jarrah (water vessel)

8. Makhazin (storehouse)
9. Rahah (palm)
10. Suffah (to be seated in a line)
11. Sukkar
12. Sharab (sweet cold drink)
13. Sifr

Exercise 2

It takes a village to raise a child. Yes indeed! People in Arab communities and villages have cooperated in raising children for generations. In the Arab world, parental responsibility does not stop with one's own children.

Hospitality is another Arab tradition. Arabs are known for enjoying a well-planned feast. Guests may also be invited to potlucks to share fellowship and stories well into the night.

Read the following story and respond to the questions below.

In a California college town, the Arab community holds a monthly potluck dinner. It is an occasion for the local Arab community to get together, and Arab students from the campus are invited. Halfway through the evening one night, two new students, Nuha from Tunisia and Nisreen from Jordan, went into the backyard. Few others noticed and went on with their conversation and munching. Those who knew the two women also knew why they went outside—both smoked cigarettes. Dr. Amin, the host and a professor from Egypt, realized what Nuha and Nisreen were up to and followed them into the backyard. He told them, "You shouldn't be smoking. You know this is bad for you. Just because you are away from home doesn't mean there is no father around here. I am your father around here." Nuha and Nisreen came back into the room, giggling and red-faced.

1. What things in this story are common in the United States and what things seem distinctive?

2. How has coming to the United States changed what it means to be Arab for Tunisian Nuha, Jordanian Nisreen, and Egyptian Dr. Amin?

Cultural close-up

The following is a small glimpse of Arab culture.

Social status

Though there is much diversity across the Arab world, we can make some general statements about social status. In Arab nations, social status is almost completely inherited, a given that is generally not questioned. Most of these nations have three social classes. The upper class may include royalty, influential families, and wealthy persons. The middle class includes government employees (including military), teachers, and those who, though not wealthy, are prosperous. The lower class is made up of both urban and rural poor. The relative status and size of these classes varies across Arab nations depending on the country's size and wealth.

1. List ways in which ideas and practices in the United States related to social classes are the same or different.

Cultural contributions

The following are just a few contributions of Arab culture. (Go online or to the library to see what else you can find out.)

- Arts: Some of the oldest examples of art have been found in the Arab world. These include tomb paintings, mosaics, rugs, blown

glass, and embroidery. Henna, gaining popularity throughout the United States for skin decoration as well as hair color, is a traditional art form in Yemen, North Africa, and Palestine.

- Numeric system: Arabic numerals were derived from a Hindu numeric system.
- Medicine: Europe learned about Arabic medicine during the Crusades of the 11th and 12th centuries. Al-Canun, a medical encyclopedia developed by the Persian Ibn Sina, who trained and worked in Baghdad, was translated into Latin and became the West's major medical text for more than five centuries.

The Arab world:

- Consists of Muslims, Christians, Jews, and others.

The Muslim world:

- There are about one billion Muslims in the world.
- About one-fifth of the world's Muslims (about 200 million) are Arabs. About 80 percent of Muslims are not Arab but are people from Africa, the Indian subcontinent, and Southeast Asia, including Iran, Turkey, Pakistan, Afghanistan, India, Indonesia, China, and the former Soviet Union.

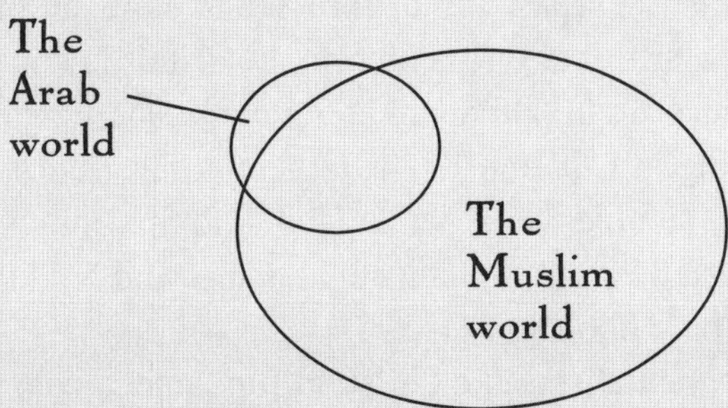

Islam

Most Arabs are Muslim, and about one-fourth of Arab Americans are Muslim. Islam started in the city of Mecca, Saudi Arabia, the birthplace of the prophet Muhammad who, it is believed, received the word of God during 610 C.E. and continuing until 632, the year of his death. The Qur'an (which means "recitation") is a record of these revelations. In addition to the Qur'an, the *Haddith* and *Shari'a* are also important to Islamic believers. The Haddith records the prophet Muhammed's words and deeds; the Shari'a, Islamic law. Islam, like Judaism and Christianity, teaches that there is one God. *Allah*—a word that Muslims, Jews, and Christians all use—means "God" in Arabic. *Islam* comes from the word meaning "peace" and means "submission" to the will of God.

Islam, like Christianity and Judaism, has different branches, *Sunni* and *Shiite* (or *Shi'a*) being the main ones. After Muhammad's death, the Muslim community disagreed about how to choose a successor. Sunni Muslims thought that the new leader should be elected; Shiites, that the new leaders should be a descendant of Muhammad. About 85 percent of the world's Muslims are Sunni. Iran, not an Arab country, is the most important Shiite nation. Shiite Muslims also live in Lebanon, southern Iraq, and other areas of the Arabian Gulf. A much smaller but important branch of Islam is the *Druze,* which grew out of an 11th-century reform movement in Egypt. One main reform was the separation of church and state, an important idea today as countries and localities apply Islamic law in different ways and degrees. Today there are about one million Druze members worldwide, living in Lebanon, Syria, Israel, Jordan, Central and South America, the Philippines, Europe, Canada, and the United States. All three of these groups follow Islam's five pillars and hold the Qur'an as their prime holy book.

Islamic fundamentalism, like Christian fundamentalism, is a reaction against cultural assaults on traditional values. In the Arab

Acts of Worship: The Five Pillars of Islam:

- *Shahada*—The confession that "there is no god but God, and Muhammad is his messenger."
- *Salat,* or prayer—Islamic teaching commands followers to pray five times daily at dawn, noon, midafternoon, sunset, and nightfall. The regular time for congregational worship and prayer is Friday noon.
- *Zakat,* or charity—All things belong to God who commands human beings to share.
- *Soum,* or fasting—Islam teaches fasting during Ramadan, the ninth month of the lunar calendar. Fasting is from sunup to sundown unless one is unable due to pregnancy, nursing, illness, weakness, or travel. Ramadan is a time of reflection, particularly on the needs of those who regularly go hungry.
- *Hajj,* or pilgrimage—The 12th month of the lunar year is the time for pilgrimage to Mecca, the birthplace of the prophet Muhammad. Most pilgrims wear simple white clothing meant to erase class and culture distinctions—all are equal before God.

world, Islamic fundamentalism is in large part a rejection of Western values that have come with the globalization and migration affecting most of the world, particularly urban areas. Because Islam is not a religion limited to specific times and places in one's life but very much a guide to living and a part of everyday life, religious practice comes in direct conflict with increasing Western secular practices. Islamic reform movements struggle with this conflict, attempting to find an alternative to fundamentalism that can renew Islam in a changing context.

Christianity in the Arab world

In 1054 C.E., the "Great Schism" split Christianity into Roman Catholicism and the Eastern Orthodox churches, which include, for example, the Coptic Orthodox Church, the Greek Orthodox Church, and the Syrian Orthodox Church. Most Christians in the Arab world belong to one of the "Eastern Rite" churches. Catholic "denominations" in the Arab world include the Maronite and Melkite churches. Protestant groups include Presbyterians, Episcopalians, and Lutherans. Orthodox, Maronite, and Melkite branches of Christianity originated in the Arab world. European missionaries in the 19th century brought European Catholicism and Protestantism. Though Christians are a small minority in the Arab world, about 65-75 percent of Arab Americans are Christians. These Arab Christians are more likely to be Catholic or Orthodox than Protestant.

Islam and Christianity

The prophet Muhammad was very aware of the Bible. Islam has great respect for key features of the Christian faith. Jesus is one of the prophets held in very high regard by all Muslims. He is mentioned in the Qur'an 80 times. The Islamic faith teaches that Jesus will return before the day of judgment. Jesus will prepare people, both the living and the dead, for Allah to judge them.

The major differences between Christianity and Islam are:

- The divinity of Jesus. It is inconceivable in Islam that the creator of the heavens and the earth will have a son. The idea of Jesus' divine sonship is not accepted in Islam.
- The crucifixion. Islam believes that Jesus was not crucified but ascended to heaven. One who looked liked him was crucified in his place because of the great love God had for Jesus.
- The Holy Trinity. Islam does not accept this teaching.

On hospitality

1. If you were going to visit a mosque, what would be your concerns and apprehensions? What greeting and hospitality would you hope for?

2. If you were going to visit a church in another country where you were not fluent in the language, what would be your concerns and apprehensions? What greeting or hospitality would you hope for?

3. What are ways that your congregation can be more hospitable to: (a) people who have never been to church before, and (b) new immigrants who are not fluent in English?

What's next

Learn about a culture by eating its food! Divide the tasks of preparing a meal for your next session. Take responsibility for the recipes on pages 49-50 that will make up your meal.

Closing prayer

Holy God, we pray for Muslims and Christians throughout the world. We pray for all peoples, especially today for our Arab brothers and sisters of all faiths. As you sent your Son to the world, by your Spirit send us to show your love. Amen

Going further

Activities

- Visit a museum with holdings from the Arab world.
- Listen to recordings by Arab musicians, including Hassan Hakmoun, Hamza El Din, Ali Jihad Racy, and Simon Shaheen.
- Learn about the philosopher Cordoba, who strongly influenced Christian theologians of the 12th to 16th centuries, including Thomas Aquinas.
- Learn about the Arab contribution to mathematics, including the invention of zero and algebra.
- With the help of videos, guest speakers, and reading, become informed about Palestine and about the relationships among Christians, Muslims, and Jews there.

Books

The Qur'an.

Bushnaq, Ina, trans., ed. *Arab Folktales.* New York: Pantheon, 1990.

Farlee, Robert. *Honoring Our Neighbor's Faith.* Minneapolis: Augsburg Fortress, 1999.

Haneef, Suzanne. *What Everyone Should Know about Islam and Muslims.* 14th edition. Library of Islam, 1996.

Munif, Abdelrahman. *Cities of Salt: A Novel.* New York: Vintage Books, 1989.

Answers to Exploration Exercise 1 on pages 40-41: 1. alcove; 2. algebra; 3. artichoke; 4. barrio; 5. coffee; 6. cotton; 7. jar; 8. magazine; 9. racket; 10. sofa; 11. sugar; 12. syrup; 13. zero.

Recipes

Baba Ghannooj (6-8 servings)

2 medium eggplants
1 tablespoon (15 ml) finely chopped parsley
1 large clove garlic, chopped
2 tablespoons (30 ml) olive oil
juice of 2 lemons
¼ cup (.06 l) tahini
¼ teaspoon (2 ml) salt

Prick eggplants in three or four places so they won't burst. Roast them in a 350° F (180° C) oven for ½ hour. Cool, peel, and cut into chunks. Put all ingredients, except the oil, in a blender. Blend for 3 minutes. Pour in a dish. Pour oil on top. Decorate with parsley. Serve with pita bread or as a salad.

Hummus

1 can garbanzo beans, drained
1 clove garlic
4 tablespoons (60 ml) tahini
¼ cup (.06 l) lemon juice
salt

In food processor, puree beans and garlic until they form a fine paste. Add remaining ingredients. Mix well. Serve with pita bread as a dip or as a salad.

Tabbouleh

3 large tomatoes, diced fine
½ cup (.12 l) olive oil
2 tablespoons (60 ml) cracked wheat, soaked in lemon juice for 1 hour
salt
1 large cucumber
4 green onions, diced fine
1 bunch parsley, washed and finely chopped
1 bunch fresh mint, washed and finely chopped

Mix all ingredients well, serve cold.

Roasted Leg of Lamb

1 leg of lamb
¼ teaspoon (1.25 ml) pepper
10 cloves garlic, crushed
¼ teaspoon (1.25 ml) nutmeg
½ teaspoon (2.5 ml) allspice
1 teaspoon dried or fresh rosemary
½ teaspoon (2.5 ml) cinnamon
salt to taste

Mix together spices with garlic. Pierce the meat with a knife in many places. Stuff the piercings with spices. Bake in preheated 450° F (230° C) oven for 1 hour. Reduce heat to 350° F (180° C). Bake 2 more hours or until meat is tender. Serve with roasted potatoes or a rice dish.

Sesame Seed Cookies

2 tablespoons (30 ml) honey
8 tablespoons (120 ml) sugar
1 tablespoon (15 ml) water
juice of ½ lemon
2 cups (0.5 l) sesame seeds, toasted

Cook the honey, sugar, water, and lemon juice until a drop put in cold water becomes a firm ball but not hard. Add sesame seeds and mix well. Transfer the mixture to a well-greased cookie tray. Roll mixture with a rolling pin and cut into diamond shapes. Let set until firm.

Harriseh

2 cups (0.5 l) smeed (farina)
1 teaspoon (5 ml) baking powder
1 cup (.24 l) sugar
3 teaspoons (15 ml) tahini
1 cup (.24 l) plain yogurt
Syrup (see recipe below)

Mix smeed, sugar, and yogurt together. Add the baking powder; mix well. Brush baking pan with the tahini. Then add the mixture. Bake at 350° F (180° C) for ½ hour or until brown. Let cool. Then cut in 3" (8 cm) squares. Add the hot syrup.

Syrup—mix 1 cup (.24 l) water, 2 cups (0.5 l) sugar, and a few drops of lemon juice in a sauce pan. Boil 15 minutes.

4

Our Arab Neighbors

Overview

An important part of hospitality is learning about those who are strangers to us. You have begun to learn about the Arab world, peoples, culture, and religions.

In this session, you will:

- learn about Arab people in the United States, especially in your neighborhood.
- identify with some of the situations Arab people face in the United States.
- plan specific ways to show hospitality to Arab neighbors.

Preparation for facilitator

Read the entire session ahead of time and gather the materials. If you will not have enough time to use all the materials presented in this session, see the introduction for suggestions about how to decide what portions to use.

In preparation for this session, the facilitator or a member of the group who likes using the Internet will need to gather some census information at www.census.gov. You will need copies of some 2000 census data to distribute for Exercise 2 in the "Exploration" section. You can get that data by going to the census Web site and searching the census of population for "Arab" and "Arab ancestry" and by searching for social and economic characteristics, or visit the Arab American Institute's Web site at www.aaiusa.org for reports on Arab American demographics. (At the time this book was written, the 2000 census data on Arab Americans was not yet available.)

Materials

For this session, each group member will need a copy of this study, a Bible, and a pen or pencil. The facilitator will also need a map of your city or metropolitan area, chart paper or a writing board, and markers.

Opening

Over the course of these sessions, you have kept a journal that has perhaps included references to Bible stories about hospitality, encounters with Arab persons (or, if you are Arab, encounters in which you became aware of being Arab), and newspaper or television stories about the Arab world or Arab peoples.

1. Share things you have observed or learned that can help you and others to be good friends to Arab neighbors.

2. Record this list on a board or chart paper. (Suggestion: Share this list with your congregation's hospitality, fellowship, outreach, or evangelism task groups.)

Pray together aloud:

Dear God, be among us as we welcome one another. Open our hearts this day to our Arab neighbors and their struggles as they make this community their home. Especially open our hearts and minds to the changes that can make us partners in this community. We pray in Jesus' name. Amen

Community building

In groups of two or three, share with one another your responses to the following questions.

1. When did you move into the neighborhood where you currently live? Why did you pick the neighborhood? What were some of the first things you noticed when you moved in?

2. When you moved in, what specific words, actions, or other things made you feel welcomed or unwelcomed? What did you do to make yourself a part of the neighborhood?

3. If you have always lived in the neighborhood where you live now, share how you have felt when newcomers have arrived. What did you first notice about them? What did you do or say to make them feel welcomed or unwelcomed? What did they do to make themselves a part of the neighborhood?

Bible study

Have someone read Luke 24:12-43 aloud. Then have volunteers read or ad lib the story in a role play, playing the parts of a narrator, the two travelers on the way to Emmaus, Jesus, and the disciples (11, if you have enough people). Mark out locations for the role play: Jerusalem, Emmaus, the road between them, the home of the two

travelers in Emmaus, and the place where the 11 are gathered in Jerusalem. (It might take some time to get ready for the role play.)

Following the role play, use these questions for discussion:

1. Whom do you see as the guest(s) in the story? (You may see more than one way to respond to this.) Explain your responses.

2. Whom do you see as the host(s) in the story? (Here, too, you may see things in more than one way.) Explain your responses.

3. What did the guests give to the hosts? What did the hosts give to the guests? How would you compare what each received?

4. How was listening a part of the hospitality shown on the parts of both guests and hosts?

The book *Cross-Cultural Evangelism: Helping Congregations Reach Out* (Nancy Maeker, Augsburg Fortress, 1993) discusses the following keys to listening and hearing another person. These keys have been developed by Michael Cobbler, an Evangelical Lutheran Church in America (ELCA) pastor:

- Seek to understand. Make every effort to appreciate what the person is saying.
- Have the attitude of a learner. Remember that a person created in God's image is telling you this story. This is indeed an opportunity to listen and hear.
- Allow the other person to frame the conversation. Do not force your own agenda into the conversation.
- Ask open-ended questions. (Open-ended questions can't be answered "yes" or "no.") Address aspects of the conversation that can open up new avenues of sharing. Beware of prying or encouraging another to tell more than what is comfortable. Boundaries need to be respected.
- Reflect on the conversation. Take notes afterward to enable you to remember significant parts of the conversation.

5. What questions do the characters in Luke 24:12-43 ask? What role do the questions play in the conversation?

6. How can asking questions be a part of showing hospitality?

7. Read aloud Psalm 137:1-6. The ancient Israelites sang this lament while in exile. Rephrase these verses in your own words. What feelings do they describe? What feelings do they evoke in you? Though the experience of the ancient Israelites in exile may not be directly comparable to most people who immigrate to the United States, immigrants experience the loss of familiar sights and sounds, home, traditions, and language. In many of our family histories, there is some experience of exile or immigration. Share with one another such experiences or memories you may have.

8. Read 1 Peter 2:11-12. Rephrase these verses in your own words. Though most Arabs in the United States are Christians, they—like most immigrants—can feel like "aliens" in the United States. Rephrase the verses to reflect advice someone might give to immigrants in a new culture with values different from their own.

9. Now, putting together your discussion about listening and asking questions with your discussion about immigrant experiences, list some open-ended questions you might ask to show hospitality to someone who has recently immigrated to the United States.

Exploration

Exercise 1

Read about George Khoury. Then break into groups of four or five for discussion using the questions that follow.

George Khoury may have moved in down the street from you. He is most likely an American citizen and there is more than a 50 percent likelihood that he was born in the United States. He speaks English very well but you may have heard him speak Arabic to members of his immediate family. George is married and has two children. An electrical engineer, he grew up in another state and moved to this area for professional reasons. He works in a small firm in the city. George's wife is also a university graduate but has chosen to stay home with their young children. They speak a mixture of English and Arabic to each other and to their friends. George and his family are Orthodox Christians. Although they go to the Orthodox Church that serves the metropolitan area, it is located at some distance from their home. They have begun to attend worship services in your church occasionally so that their children can attend Sunday school regularly.

1. Can you imagine George and his family becoming active in your church? Why or why not?

2. What will make George and his family feel welcome or unwelcome in your congregation?

Exercise 2

Look at the 2000 census data on Arab Americans for the nation and your community. See page 52 for details on obtaining this information. Then respond to these questions.

1. Where are the largest concentrations of Arab American population?

2. From what countries have Arabs come to the United States?

3. What are their occupations?

4. What is their level of education?

5. What is the average income of an Arab American household?

Take a look at a map of your town, city, or metropolitan area.

6. If possible, identify the various ethnic and language groups you are aware of and where they live. (If you are not sure, think about where there are particular ethnic businesses, schools, restaurants, or other organizations.)

7. If possible, note specifically the areas where Arab people live.

8. Which of the ethnic and language groups are represented at your workplace or school? In your neighborhood? In your congregation? In other organizations or groups to which you belong?

9. What is your congregation's geographic relationship to the areas where Arab Americans live?

10. What is your congregation's social relationship to the areas where Arab Americans live? What does that imply about your congregation's social relationship to the people themselves?

Cultural close-up

Arabs have been in North America for hundreds of years, probably arriving as early as the 15th century with Spanish explorers. Significant Arab immigration began in the late 19th century along with great migration from Europe. The 1890s witnessed the first Arabic language newspaper in the United States and three Arab churches in New York. In 1923, Highland Park, Michigan, had the first Arab mosque in the United States. It is estimated that by 1924, about 200,000 Arabs lived in the United States, mostly Christians from Syria and Lebanon, many from rural areas and with little formal education. Early Arab immigrants, like other ethnic groups, came to this country for economic and educational opportunities. They settled primarily in cities in the Northeast and Midwest.

Beginning in the 1920s, quotas regulated immigration to the United States except from northern and western Europe. The most important change in Arab immigration was a shift to Palestinians displaced from their homeland by Jewish immigrant resettlement in Palestine following World War I. In 1936, Palestinians were for the first time the largest Arab immigrant group to the United States. In 1965, U.S. immigration policies again opened the doors to immigrants. Between 1965 and 1992, 360,000 of the total 400,000 Arab immigrants to the United States came from Lebanon, Jordan/ Palestine, Egypt, Iraq, Syria, and Yemen. Today there are more than three million Arab Americans in the United States. In 1995, the largest Arab American populations were in California, New York, Michigan, Florida, Illinois, New Jersey, Massachusetts, Texas, Ohio, and Pennsylvania. At that time, it was estimated that 40 percent of the Arab American population was made up of first-generation immigrants, that is, people who were born in the Arab world and immigrated to the United States.

Today, Arab Americans are found in a wide variety of occupations. A 1994 study estimated that 60 percent of Arab Americans work as executives, professionals, salespeople, administrative support personnel, and service personnel. The distribution of Arab Americans in particular job categories varies from place to place. For example, in major manufacturing cities like Detroit and Chicago, Arab Americans, like many others, are likely to work in manufacturing, in contrast to Boston, where Arab Americans, along with others, are more likely to be employed in education and health care jobs. According to John Zogby ("Arab Americans," in *Race and Ethnic Relations,* 11th ed., McGraw-Hill/Dushkin, 2001), Arab Americans have the highest per capita ownership of businesses of any ethnic group in the United States.

Arab Americans place a high value on education and learning. This is part of a centuries-old tradition in Arab cultures. While the majority of Arab Americans were born in the United States and therefore

speak English as a first language, those who immigrate may face challenges in public education settings. Some public schools offer bilingual support, if not bilingual classrooms. What is the practice in your area?

Along with language, other cultural factors make for diversity in public education settings. For example, Muslim children celebrate different holidays, eat somewhat different foods, and wear different garb than others. In some communities, Arab American Muslims have established private Islamic schools that include standard public school curriculum plus religion and Arabic. Is there an Islamic school in your neighborhood?

Arab Americans tend to be more highly educated than the average person in the United States, more likely to attend college, more likely to obtain graduate degrees, and less likely to be unemployed. Almost a third of Arab Americans have annual incomes of more than $75,000.

Palestine—A special concern

When Israel was created in 1948, many Palestinians became refugees and now live in exile in Arab countries. Between 1965 and 1992, most Palestinian immigrants to the United States were from Jerusalem and the West Bank. According to a Zogby International study completed in 2000 ("Arab Americans," Arab American Institute, 2000), the Middle East—particularly the Arab-Israeli conflict—is a major concern to Arab Americans, both immigrants and those born in the United States. Most Arab Americans (87.2 percent) agree that there should be an independent Palestinian state. In addition to securing the rights of Palestinians, other important issues to Arab Americans regarding the Middle East are: the sovereignty of Lebanon, normalized relations between the United States and Arab

countries, the status of Jerusalem, and promotion of human rights in the Arab world.

Three contradictory agreements from the early 20th century have contributed to current conflicts:

- Sherif Hysayn-McMahon Correspondence (1915-16). In this correspondence, Great Britain agreed to support an Arab revolt that would weaken the Ottoman Empire. In return, the Arabs would achieve their independence.
- Sykes Picot Agreement (1916). In this pact, the Arab world was divided between Great Britain and France. France gained control over Syria and Lebanon; Britain, over Iraq, Jordan, and Palestine.
- Balfour Declaration (1917). This agreement between the British and Jewish nationalists (Zionists) stated that the British government viewed favorably "the establishment of a Jewish homeland in Palestine." Palestinian Arabs—90 percent of the population of Palestine at that time—were not named in or consulted about this declaration.

After World War II, Arab states began to gain independence. In 1947, the United Nations decided to establish a safe homeland for Jews. The United Nations divided Palestine, establishing a Jewish state and an Arab state. Half of Palestine, including the most fertile land, was given to Jews, who made up one-third of the population and had owned about a fifth of the land. The other half was designated for Palestinian Arabs, who had owned most of the land. The Israelis won the war that ensued. More than 800,000 Palestinians lost their homes and livelihoods; many became refugees. The Israelis also won subsequent wars in 1956, 1967, 1973, and 1982. By 1967, Israel occupied all of Palestine and also parts of Egypt and Syria.

The American-Arab Anti-Discrimination Committee, the Arab American Institute, and the Association of Arab-American University Graduates are among the national organizations that monitor Middle East policy and events and provide information on Arab concerns.

Arab Christian traditions

About half of Arab Americans are Christians. Most are Orthodox Christians, members of some of the very oldest Christian denominations in the world.

■ Though most Arab American Christians celebrate Christmas on December 25, the traditional Orthodox Christmas celebration is on January 6, or Epiphany.

■ Three weeks before Lent, Chaldean and Assyrian Americans who are Catholics from Iraq and Syria celebrate God's sending of the prophet Jonah to the people of Nineveh.

■ Easter is the most important holiday for Arab Christians.

On hospitality

1. Begin to pray regularly in your congregation about your relationships with and hospitality to Arab Americans. Pray publicly in worship and in smaller groups and meetings of congregation members. Ask members to pray at home and in other personal prayers.

2. Write a brief, focused prayer that can be used in these varied settings. Here are some possibilities to consider in writing your own prayer.

- ■ Teach us, O God, what it means to be good neighbors and help us to be good neighbors to our Arab American brothers and sisters.
- ■ Holy Spirit, lead us into relationships with our Arab American neighbors and give us words of hospitality wherever you lead.
- ■ Jesus, fill us with your love in our relationships with Arab Americans.

What's next

1. Brainstorm a list of specific ways that your congregation can be neighborly and hospitable to Arab neighbors. Remember that in brainstorming there are no wrong answers. Let your imagination go—but think very particularly about your congregation, its gifts, and its setting.

2. Once you have developed a list, choose one or two items and make specific plans for neighborliness and hospitality.

Here's a list of suggestions to get you started.

- Plan an evening of cultural awareness to educate the congregation about the Arab world and your Arab neighbors.
- Invite a community leader to address the congregation in an informal setting about some aspect of Arab history, culture, politics, or religions.
- Devote a month of Sunday school sessions to developing cultural awareness about Arab Americans. Ask young and old alike to invite friends of Arab descent from school and work. Ask the guests to share their experiences as Arab Americans.
- Schedule a time when members from your congregation can visit and worship in a predominantly Arab American congregation. Contact the pastor ahead of time to plan your visit. Perhaps you can also arrange a social time.
- Contact the American-Arab Anti-Discrimination Committee (www.adc.com) to learn what you can do. Make a commitment to help alleviate discrimination against Arab Americans.
- Set aside time for a series of Christian-Muslim dialogues. Invite a local Islamic religious leader or teacher and other Muslims to participate in conversation with you.
- Obtain copies of *Cross-Cultural Evangelism: Helping Congregations Reach Out* (Augsburg Fortress, 1993, ISBN 6-0000-0864-3) and develop a plan for outreach to your Arab neighbors.

Closing prayer

Almighty God, we know that you have broken the barriers between us through Jesus Christ. We pray that you will help us to welcome our Arab neighbors. We are unsure of ourselves, but we trust that you will teach us how to be with one another. We pray this in the name of Jesus the Christ who lives and reigns with you forever. Amen

Going further

Books

Ameri, Anan and Dawn Ramey, eds. *Arab American Encyclopedia.* Detroit: Arab Community Center for Economic and Social Service (ACCESS), 2000.

Cainkar, Louise. *Meeting Community Needs, Building on Community Strengths.* Chicago: Arab American Action Network, 1998.

McCarus, Ernest, ed. *The Development of Arab-American Identity.* Ann Arbor: University of Michigan Press, 1994.

Suleiman, Michael, ed. *Arabs in America: Building a New Future.* Philadelphia: Temple University Press, 2000.

Organizations

The Association of Arab-American University Graduates (AAUG) and the National Association of Arab Americans (NAAA) are among the organizations that monitor Middle East policy and events, provide information and education, and promote Arab concerns.

Videos

Benatt Chicago (Daughters of Chicago): Growing Up Arab and Female in Chicago, directed and produced by Jennifer Bing-Canar and Mary Zerkel. Chicago: American Friends Service Committee, 1996.

Tales from Arab Detroit, directed by Joan Mandell and produced by the Arab Community Center for Economic and Social Services (ACCESS) and Sally Howell. Ho-Ho-Kus, N.J.: New Day Films, 1995.

Web sites

www.adc.com (American-Arab Anti-Discrimination Committee)
www.aaiusa.org (Arab American Institute)
www.ArabChat.com (ArabChat)
www.Arabic-words.com (Arab Zone)